I thank God everyday for bringing you into my life

A special gift

for

Debbie - My Bestest Friend

from

JeRRie

date

12-25-07

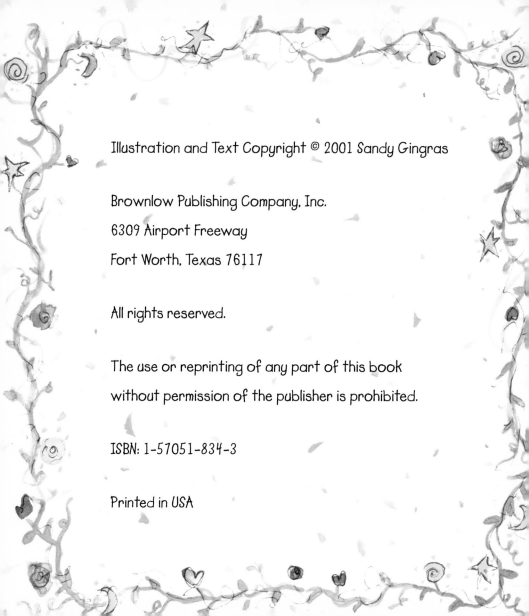

Brownlow Publishing Company, Inc.

6309 Airport Freeway

Fort Worth, Texas 76117

ISBN: 1-57051-834-3

Printed in USA

To doLLy and biLLy

for Their Love and LighT

My first friend was invisible. She lived in our kitchen pantry between the cereal boxes. She was bratty and free in every way that I wanted to be. I brought her my best stories and favorite marbles, and she turned everything on the shelves upside down and got me into trouble.

From her, I learned that a friend changes you invisibly. She got me to whisper secrets from way down in my heart, showed me how to laugh about nothing, how to listen to what wasn't said. She taught me how the best things in life are simple and right next to us and are often the hardest to see.

how To be a friend

Written and iLLusTraTed by Sandy Gingras

share

Brownlow

To risk The chancy
Times of Sun
and rain

and become buds.

To Commit To some common ground but

To blossom into difference

Friendship is a going ahead with no map on a journey full of twisty turns, loop-de-loops, dead ends and detours.

ALLow for ups and downs.

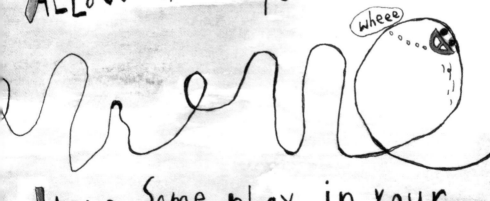

wheee

Have some play in your steering wheel

coast

when you can

SaVor SweeT SiLences

and

Bask in The Sunny Spots

They make iT aLL worThwhiLe.

forgive

with grace

Learn how to bounce

Know when To
LeT things sLide...
the
pasT
whaT
we
said
hard
feeLings

and To remember when...

LighT a way home

friend
ship

when Life geTs dark

Any gesture of heart
(no matter how small)
radiates out

and Touches us all

Like the opposite of gravity, friendship is a force that lifts us...

and supports us.

When Life unravels...
a friend pushes...
LeT's go
and paTs...
There, There.
and heLps us shine again.

A friendship is a
baLancing.

It's an up and
downing business.

ENdurance counTs.

duck

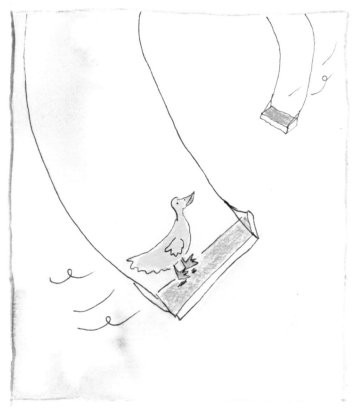

during mood swings

a friend knows when To dig down deep

when To celebrate The superficial

A friend knows That some WaLLS are for keeping

and Some WaLLS are for LeTTing go.

Friendship

is what we build

and rebuild...

...even beTTer

they know the value

# of a good drift

they erase

dear friend,
you really
sh ould
you are soo...

judgment,

and use LaughTer

as a SofTening agent

and
just allowing you

heart
at
rest

To be.

A friend is where

Welcome

You're safe and at home.

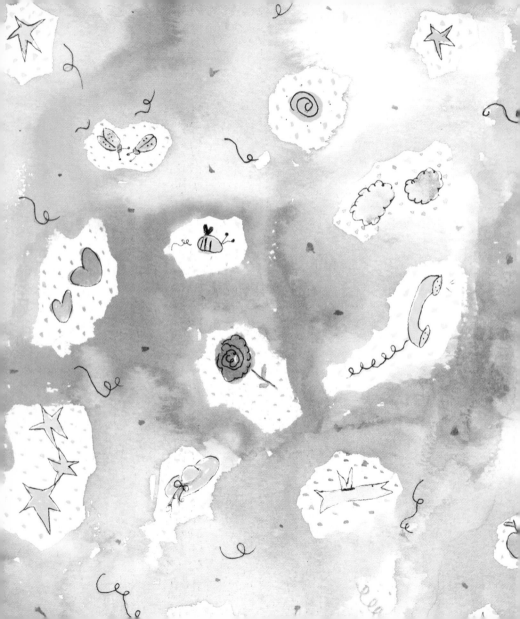